MW01118351

Life through the Rhythm and rhyme of Poetry

Let Go and…
Hold On!!!

Let Go of Brokenness
Let Healing Begin

Antonina Caprino Bell

ISBN 978-1-68517-626-6 (paperback)
ISBN 978-1-68517-627-3 (digital)

Christian Faith Publishing
832 Park Avenue
Meadville, PA 16335
www.christianfaithpublishing.com

All Scripture quotations are from the Holy Bible, New American Standard Version

Printed in the United States of America

DEDICATION

To my problems, I say... *Thank You!*
Thank you for forcing me to draw deep within myself—
I'm discovering who I am
Thank you for pushing me hard into my spiritual quest—
I'm discovering who God is
Thank you for the wounds and the heartaches—
I'm discovering compassion
Thank you for giving me the privilege to be unhappy—
I'm discovering I have choices
Thank you for the loneliness and the misery—
I'm discovering I am one with humanity
Thank You!!!!

Contents

Let Go of Control... Hold On To Your MARRIAGE

Introduction

Who am I? Who are you? What are the traumas that have formed emotional and psychological patterns in us that make us feel stuck? It takes time to discover the patterns that have shaped our lives and the buttons that control us. If the addictions we experience in our society are any indication of the dysfunction of our world, we can be sure that the roots go deep into the fabric of our human condition.

As children, we think that our parents are supposed to be our protectors. In many cases, parents think they are doing the right thing but in reality, they do not realize that they are harming their children. There are many who have been wounded and face challenges—especially inside of relationships. As we grow into teens and adults, we look for that "one" that will complete us—fulfill us; but, two wounded people cannot come together and expect to live in harmony.

The important thing is: what are we going to do about it? It is not easy to confront that wounded person inside of us that put up with so much and required so little. On the road to recovery we have to be aware of how we are showing up. We don't grow by just complaining about what has happened to us. We grow through self-inquiry. The truth is that we have to come to a place of complete abandonment—let go of self and all its pitfalls and choose life—holding on to that which is selfless.

For 45 years I have poured my heart out through writing. It served as a mirror to see and feel the real me—the "me" I was deep down inside. Writing showed me clearly the places I was getting stuck. It especially showed me the buttons that were pushed by those I was always trying to please. So many times, I hungered for affirmation. Why was I never enough? I just wanted to learn how to overcome my shortcomings.

Through the years, I realized I was emotionally immature and ignorant about many things. When a challenge was before me, I was unable to rise up and face that challenge. As I stepped back to look at myself and the emotions that always tried to control, I saw how deeply I could get entangled with the superficial and not understand the roots of bitterness that could hold, bind and control me.

The dysfunction all goes back to a deep sense of abandonment and always feeling disconnected as far back as I can remember. It would be nice to say that I came from a healthy home and my parents modeled unconditional love. Instead, I grew up feeling that love is conditional. I grew up under very controlling parents, feeling guilted and ashamed, feeling criticized and very often physically abused.

As we grew into adults, my mother pitted her children against each other and my father's answer was always, "Forget about it." I don't fault my parents. They did the best they could. They just didn't have the tools in their emotional storehouse to impart life to their children. In fact, both parents were very narcissistic in their behaviors. The hunger for love and attention was never fulfilled as a child. No matter how hard I tried, I could never please my parents.

I've met many people through the years that had far worse childhoods than me; I am simply someone who is trying to understand herself and maybe offer encouragement to those of you who can relate. I came to the realization that it was me, not anyone else, that needed to be transformed.[1] It is of no use to point the finger and put the blame on others and our circumstances—that just keeps us stuck.

This book is not a "woe is me" story, but it is about the pain that brought me to a spiritual path when I was just in my mid 20's—a path that revealed the wounded places deep down inside of me. Through the years, I have emerged not only knowing the love of God that set me free but getting to know myself—who I am and "whose" I am.

---

[1] *Romans 12:2 "And do not be conformed to this world, but be transformed by the renewing of your mind, so that you may prove what the will of God is, that which is good and acceptable and perfect.*

These poems are my stories—the stories that shaped my life. Much like the potter who smashes down the clay creation to start all over again, the Master Potter used people to bring me to an end of my emotionally crippled self and to bring me to a place of awareness and willingness to let it all go. Walk with me through these pages and read about my struggles and my victories.

We can make peace with the past and we can affect our future. Wisdom is needed.[2] The Serenity Prayer states so beautifully, "God grant me the serenity to accept the things I cannot change; courage to change the things I can; and wisdom to know the difference."[3]

These are the stories of finding strength through weakness and discovering purpose in life. I soon learned that every difficult circumstance of my life that was meant for evil, God turned for my good.[4] Through it all, I have realized that my confidence would come as I walked on my spiritual path. It's not that I have arrived, "but one thing I do: forgetting what lies behind and reaching forward to what lies ahead, I press on toward the goal for the prize of the upward call of God in Christ Jesus." *(Philippians 3: 14, 15)*

There is a quote that says it beautifully, "Do everything with a mind that lets go. Don't accept praise or gain or anything else. If you let go a little, you will have a little peace. If you let go a lot, you will have a lot of peace. If you let go completely, you will know complete peace and freedom."[5]

It is time to *let go* of all the dysfunction and it is time to *hold on* to the good and the wholesome so… Let Go and… Hold On!

---

2   *Proverbs 4:7 "Wisdom is the principle thing; therefore, get wisdom; and with all thy getting, get understanding."*
    Job 12:12 "Wisdom is with the aged, and with long life comes understanding."
3   *The serenity prayer by Reinhold Niebuhr (1892-1971)*
4   *Genesis 50:20 "As for you, you meant evil against me, but God meant it for good…"*
5   *Quote by Chah Subhaddo (known in English as Ajahn Chah (1918-1992)*

Part One

Let Go of Bitterness...
Hold On To
LIFE

Beautiful Life

Life is so beautiful
So full of magic and possibilities
The storms of life are meant to come
But remember, you are never really alone

God's love is like the sun
Always there in spite of the clouds
Constant and unchanging
Sometimes hidden but there just the same

Not moveable—the earth moves
But never the sun
What can take God's love away?
What can move the sun?

We all crave for the unconditional love of another
Even when that is not there,
Can we believe beyond the clouds?
Beyond our feelings?

Feelings of abandonment, rejection
not worthy, not loved
Moving on to a new book
New chapter, new journey, new life

You *are* whole
You *are* one with God
You *are* worthy
You *are* His
You *are* valuable
You *are* able
You *are* a gift
You *are* a beautiful life!

Bitterness

What makes me feel alive and fulfilled? What makes me feel like my life is worth living? To be loved and accepted, appreciated and cared for—to experience the perfect bond of love and unity. To give is easy when it falls in the light of good and healthy relationships—together building, giving, communicating…

When communication ceases to be and unreciprocated love continues, the giving of self and love makes life more and more difficult. The constant feeling that relationships are disconnected makes life feel dark and dreary.

And the love of many will grow cold in the last days[1]. So, what is the answer? How do I stretch myself beyond expectancy and give as Jesus gave? How do I give of myself expecting nothing in return? Can I? Am I able to give with total and complete abandon? Am I able to keep on reaching out with joy and light and life?

I reach deep within and realize, "No, this is absurdity and humanly impossible." I come to the realization that by grace I stand. "His grace is sufficient,"[2] so it was spoken to me by the prophet so long ago when times were different, but the problems were the same. By grace I stand!

---

[1] *Matthew 24:12 "Because lawlessness is increased, most people's love will grow cold."*

[2] *II Corinthians 12:9 "And He said to me, 'My grace is sufficient for you, for power is perfected in weakness.'"*

Abundant Life

The divine gift from the Divine One!

Oh Life of God—come forth in me!

Come forth in me is my one plea!

Oh Love of God—so rich and pure

Help me to love and to endure

I bow to Thee oh power of Life

I realize You alone, oh Love,

Have the power to free!

So free me now—unleash Thy power

To spread Your love in this cold hour!

Life's Questions???

Does anybody really care?
Where is the compassion and the mercy?
Where is the hope and the peace?
Is there one who would be willing to walk with me?
Is there one who would be willing to hold my hand?
Who would give me a shoulder to lean on?
Is there a friend to run to when times are hard?

Questions…questions…and more questions????
Life slipping—does anyone notice?
Is anyone interested in helping me carry my load?
Or am I chasing after wind?
What is the purpose for my existence?
Children grown and gone—then what??
Where is life? What is life?

Over and over again I hear, "I love you."
I say, "I love you." What does it mean?
I find only emptiness and more questions.
Such disillusionment within me
Life is for the beautiful and the confident
I have only myself to offer—what am I?
Who am I? What does life want out of me?

When will satisfaction come?
A bottomless pit of never enough
Trickery—your main deception
Looks good…maybe this time…bottom falls out

Hope deferred once again[1]
I see the wretchedness of myself and I ask, Who??
When??... Where?... How?????

But Alas! Rise—I will—to a new day—to a new self
Have your way oh Master Potter[2]
You have a plan—there is a purpose
Go ahead, smash me down again
Rework me until nothing is left of the old self
Nothing is left of the hopes and dreams—the ego
With all its demands and lusts.

Recreate me until all that's left is You
Your work tried by fire—tested with time
Let the mark be left on those I leave behind one day
The mark of one who battled in life
One who believed beyond belief
One who persevered through weakness and inability
One who had no more questions—only the answer.

---

[1] *Proverbs 13:12 "Hope deferred makes the heart sick..."*
[2] *Isaiah 64:8 "... O Lord You are our Father, we are the clay, You are the potter..."*
Jeremiah 18:6 "... Behold like the clay in the potter's hand, so are you in My hand."
Romans 9:21 "Or does not the potter have a right over the clay..."

Diminished!

Weep on oh willow for you have cause
Your trunks and branches have fallen
Lifeless limbs drop like leaves
The winds have blown
Strong winds—powerful winds
Reducing you to a mere shadow
Of what once stood strong—immovable.

Your branches spread wide and tall
Your roots sank deep
Many came and found shelter in your shade
Fun for children along the water's edge
You are forever gone now
With only reflections and shadows
Of the glory that was once all yours.

I will always remember you, oh willow
Perhaps from a sense of oneness with you
The woman once felt strong—immovable
Diminished through the storms of life
From strength to weakness
From youth to old age
Time marches on—the end must come.

Life like nature is made up of seasons
Seasons that come and go
To everything there is a season
A time for every purpose under heaven[1]

---

[1] *Ecclesiastes 3:1 "There is an appointed time for everything…"*

He has made everything beautiful in its time[2]
Nothing meant to last forever
But the fruit of the precious seeds will go on.

---

[2]   *Ecclesiastes 3:11 "He hath made everything beautiful in his time."* (KJV)

A Bruised Reed

People ready—always ready to condemn—to accuse
Always wanting to cast their righteous stones
She is right beside Him now
He seems so different than her accusers
She wonders what is it about Him…
She feels loved and secure—very secure by His side

The words of Isaiah ring in her ears,
"He will not crush the weakest reed
Or put out a flickering candle
He will bring justice to all who have been wronged."[1]
The tears fall as He touches her with His pure love
So much softness in His voice,
"Woman where are they? Did no one condemn you?"

She cries, Lord forgive me for I have sinned
I am weary Lord but somehow you have refreshed me
Would you help me to overcome the loneliness?
The temptations, the rejections?
I need Your help, my Lord, I cannot make it alone
I must know You are here with me, beside me
Forgive me—make me whole Lord for I am weak
I stumble easily.

"I do not condemn you either
Go. From now on sin no more."[2]

---

[1] *Isaiah 42:3 "A bent reed He will not break off and a dimly burning wick He will not extinguish; He will faithfully bring forth justice."*
[2] *John 8:3 "Then the scribes and Pharisees brought a woman who had been caught in adultery and made her stand in the middle."*

His reassurance comes and she is like a
weaned child content to be without
Content to be neglected, condemned, rejected
For it is with compassion that He draws her to His side
He speaks as one who knows, one who understands
One who would lay down His life.

It is here that strength comes
She is free to live and move and exist[3]
As peace floods her soul, she is refreshed in His love
As she looks to Him, her heart is comforted
She is free—a free woman
It is well with her soul for the Life-Giver has come
He extinguished all the flaming arrows of the evil one[4]
She is loved, she is accepted, she is whole.

He is making a way where there was no way[5]
There was no hope of ever finding life
She turns to Him and He is there for her
He holds her hands and looks into her face
With a love that is liberating
She is loved and she is blessed to know this love…
this grace…this mercy
Extended to this bruised reed, and this flickering wick…

---

[3]   *Acts 17:28 "For in him we live and move and have our being…"*
[4]   *Ephesians 6:16 "In all circumstances, hold faith as a shield, to quench all the
      flaming arrows of the evil one."*
[5]   *Isaiah 43:19 "Behold I am going to do something new, now it will spring up; will
      you not be aware of it? I will even make a roadway in the wilderness,…"*

That's Life!

Melting under the fire and pain of brokenness
Unfiltered liquid gold pouring forth[1]
Separating the dross from the essence of its purest form
Giving up, letting go of thought, of past and future
Allowing pureness of *life* in peace and joy *now*!
As it was in the beginning and ever is. *Amen*!

---

[1] *Malachi 3:3 "…and He will purify the sons of Levi and refine them like gold and silver…"*

The Princess

A little girl was born today—banner headlines and bouquets
Waves of good wishes greet this new-born princess
Wouldn't it be wonderful if each life came into the world
With such a welcome—such a cause of joy!

But some don't have a chance at all
Their lives snuffed out—it's not against the law
Millions of babies being killed
"Pro-Choice" is the mother's will

When will we awaken from this holocaust?
When will this mountain of dead babies come to haunt us?
When will we realize that life is much too precious?
To be "Pro-Life" to some is just ludicrous[1]

But what if we valued family and life?
What if we helped eliminate turmoil and strife?
People being used and abused with no end
What if we considered each one a friend?

Without the value of human life
Our world is ruled by hatred and strife?
Foundation of family seems a thing of the past
How long do you think a society can last?

No moral standards we live with today
"If it feels good do it" is the popular way

---

[1] *Deuteronomy 30:19 "… I have set before you life and death, blessings and curses. Now choose life, so that you and your children may live."*

But it's a road that leads to heartache and pain
Many broken lives are all we will gain

So, the dysfunction grows like a cancer
But with spiritual eyes we *can* find the answer
The answer is clear "Till death do us part."
What if we lived with a morally pure heart?

Saving sex within the boundaries of marriage and love
Husband and wife looking to God up above
Bringing up children so safe and secure
With love at the center of family for sure

To continue on this moral decay
Depression, suicide, addictions leading the way
Pornography, prostitution and every vice known to man
Go ahead do your own thing—destruction's the plan

But what if we each stopped long enough to see?
This was not to be man's destiny
The promise of life—if we seek, we will find[2]
Discovering the message of God for mankind!

---

[2] *Jeremiah 29:13 "You will seek me and find me when you seek me with all your heart."*

Spirit of St. Francis[1]

Arise—oh yes, Arise!
In the spirit of St. Francis, arise
A love song is being sung—can you hear it?
Not of a mortal or fleeting love
But of a divine love—supernatural
Be warmed in the sunshine of His perfect love
He asks that you love with all your heart
God's love lasts not for a moment
But for an eternity—forever and always.

A call to love is the call of Christ
What energy is awoken by the call of love?
The call of unity, the call of friendship
The call of mercy and grace
In the spirit of St. Francis to give up all
For the cause of Christ—the cause of love
"Accepting the things we cannot change
Changing the things we can
Having the wisdom to know the difference."[2]

In the spirit of St. Francis, make us a channel
The greater the love, the greater the pain
Love that could reach the world through pain
Love with its inherent goodness has to clash with evil
Evil—all forms of separateness, greediness,
Hating…hurting…slaying…despising
Love is the only reality, must be allowed to come

---

[1] *Inspired by In the Steps of St. Francis by Ernest Raymond*
[2] *The Serenity Prayer by Reinhold Niebuhr 1892-1971*

Give birth in our hearts
Grow oh love, simple love, pure love.

Let love show us the cross we must bear
Let it lead us to a place of crucifixion
The highest calling—death to ego
Complete abandonment reviving the soul
For the cause of Christ—for the cause of love
Lay down your will—lay down your life
Hoping, building together
Reaching out to one another
In the spirit of St. Francis!

The Pit

To my precious friends who struggle with addiction…

The pit is deep and dark
I hear your cries for help
You're hungry I know
I have food, I can throw it down
Into your pit, into your hole
But do I really want to keep you there?

It is love that calls you out—calls you up
Out of your hole—out of your pit
Why would you stay in that place of despair?
I will not help you stay there
I refuse to keep you in that place of
despondency—that place of death
In this pit that is as fierce as a grave
LIFE or death is the choice
Choose you this day[1]
"The blessing or the curse"
He is able to keep you and sustain you
I won't hang with you in your defeat
But I know that you can step up to His victory

It's a higher place
A peaceful place

---

[1] *Deuteronomy 30:19 "… I have placed before you life and death, the blessing and the curse. So choose life in order that you may live…"*

A place of contentment and purpose
Where mind and spirit intersect
A higher ground—this place of *life*
But it's your choice—your call

Come…all you who labor and are heavy laden…[2]
He is *The Way, The Truth*, and *The Life*[3]
Where, O death is your victory?
Where, O grave is your sting?[4]
But thanks be to God
He gives us the victory
Through our Lord Jesus Christ
Today is the day—now is the time[5]
Climb up, climb out, step out of *The Pit*
Choose LIFE!

---

[2] *Matthew 11:28 "Come to Me, all who are weary and burdened, and I will give you rest."*

[3] *John 14:6 "Jesus said to him, 'I am the way, and the truth, and the life'…"*

[4] *I Corinthians 15:55 "Where O Death, is your victory? Where, O Death is your sting."*

[5] *II Corinthians 6:2 "…now is a favorable time, behold, now is a day of salvation."*

Whole at Last

Brokenness inside, erosion outside
Shedding from within while being eroded without
By the rough hands of the world
Let go, let go, let go!
Screams everything within you.

Breathe, breathe, breathe!
Take in the clean air, the pure air
That which cleanses and purifies—makes whole
That which gives the strength of the Divine
From whom flows all love and goodness.

Come breath of God
Which causes our dead, dry bones to come alive[1]
For beautiful new skin to form[2]
Creating wholeness of life
Reaching, touching, healing,
Loving, forgiving, believing
Whole at last!!

---

[1] *Ezekiel 37:5 "… I am going to make breath enter you so that you may come to life."*
[2] *Ezekiel 37:6 "…and behold, tendons were on them, and flesh grew and skin covered them…"*

Dancing River

Looking for I don't know what,
Going I don't know where
I wait and I wait and I wait[1]
For something, for someone
Something that inspires
Someone that brings meaning

Oh meaningless life
Oh wasteland in the wild
Yield your produce—your work
Barren places shape me
Make me who I need to be

Fill me with grace and glory
Fill the empty places
Oh river of God, come!
Flow through the barrenness
Run through with dancing feet
Turning my mourning into dancing![2]

---

[1]   *Isaiah 40:31 "Yet those who wait for the Lord will gain new strength…"*
[2]   *Psalm 30:11 "You have turned my mourning into dancing for me; you have untied my sackcloth and encircled me with joy."*

Just Be

Simplicity calling me—wooing me
Gentle calming water, reflecting the beauty
Little ripples casting their silvery sheen
The birds of the air are fed
The grass of the field does not toil
The lilies are calm and serene[1]
The art of "being" is here and now
"Becoming" is always driving and hoping
To simply "be" is peace to the soul

Then why are you downcast oh my soul?
Why the constant pushing and driving?
The striving—to become what? Become who?
Be at peace, oh my soul
And peace will attend your way
Simply "be" today, tomorrow, and forever!
Let the peace of all that surrounds, overtake you
Become one with nature
"*Be*" content, "*Be*" full, "*Be*" alive…
Just "*Be*"

---

[1] *Matthew 6:28 "… Notice how the lilies of the field grow; they do not labor nor do they spin thread for cloth, yet I say to you that not even Solomon in all his glory clothed himself like one of these."*

Past, Future, NOW...

Melting under the fire and pain of bitterness
Unfiltered liquid gold pouring forth[1]
Separating the dross from the essence of its purity
Giving up, letting go of thought, of past, of future
Allowing pureness of life in peace and joy
Ready for the masterpiece—an empty canvas
Whitewashed clean by the abandonment of self—of ego
Not sure of the outcome but feeling new and clean
Ready to let go, let God
Re-think, re-new, re-store, re-born
Beyond the yesterday and tomorrow
In the *"now"* happily foreverafter

---

[1] *Proberbs 17:3 "...the furnace (is) for gold, but the Lord tests the hearts."*

Journal Entry: January 5, 2001—Facilitated a parenting workshop in a local prison full of mothers who have been taken away from their children...

Within the Bars

Their faces haunt me day and night
The eyes of those who have been rejected—
Society's castaways
Of little importance to our world
With its fast-paced and "Sorry, I don't have time" attitude[1]
Most of the time not caring to get involved
Not wishing to get entangled
With these who have been rejected and abused—
Abuse, with no end in sight.

Who will go? Who will reach out a hand?
Who will make their world a more comfortable place?
A warmer and brighter place?
A world with more compassion?
A world with more love?
Who will help their children through the pain?
From the abuse that continues like a roaring monster
Destroying generation after generation—
Destruction, passed on and on and on and on...

Arising slowly but surely from the pain of life
Probing, exploring under all the secret places
The hidden places of the soul

---

[1]   *Matthew 25:36 "... I was in prison and you came to me."*

For in the soul and the spirit is the key
It lies hidden in obscurity—
In the shadows of prison doors
Out of sight, or so it seems, but in plain view
The door is open, you are free
Free to discover, free to probe

Free to explore the gift that you are
Free from the numbing grip
The cold, hard grip of life
Free from the chains and shackles
That can hold a gentle soul
The soft, tender spirit of a woman
Weak and wounded you arise
As you arise, strength grows
And freedom comes from within the bars.

Full Speed Ahead

Sitting…waiting…idling…more waiting
Engines start…motor revs up
All systems "go" for the big ascent
Waiting for the command—the clearance
The way is clear!

Engines rev—louder—more power
Start to roll forward
Moving forward…gaining speed…
Power building
Gently lifting upwards—higher, higher

Breaking through to a brighter place
Above the clouds, Earth looks so small
Getting brighter—more light
More sun—a happy place!

Away from all that oppresses
All that keeps life out
Freeee!! Above the clouds at last
Over the rainbow—the magical place
The place of our hopes and dreams!

Though turbulent at times
Still moving forward
Not losing speed
On to my destination
Determination—full speed ahead!

Much like my life…
Sitting…waiting…idling…more waiting[1]
So much inside of me
Waiting to go forth
Dreaming…planning…hoping…

Looking to the future
But not wanting today to slip away
Need to catch up to my destiny
Mounting up—faith lifting upward
Arising and moving forward
Moving upward and onward

Need to break free—to be…
To know…to love…to be known…to be loved
To move somewhere over the rainbow—the promise
That magical place
The place of our hopes and dreams!

Though turbulent at times,
Can't lose speed—can't lose focus
Still moving forward
On to my destination
Determination—full speed ahead!

---

[1] *Isaiah 40:31 "Yet those who wait for the Lord will gain new strength; they will mount up with wings like eagles, they will run and not get tired, they will walk and not become weary."*

Part Two

Let Go of Fear...
Hold On To
FAITH

Words

Give me words, Lord
That have never been written
Words that have never been said
Words that will transform
The hardest of hearts
Words to be eaten and digested
Offering nutritious sustenance to the soul
Not that we need more words
We just need You—the True Word
Feed our souls, Oh Bread of Life!

The Preacher

It was on a Friday evening
When I heard a preacher talking
He was telling of a man his name is Jesus—
Do you know Him?
And he told of how He loves us
And He cares about our problems
And I felt God's love surround me
As I listened oh so closely
As He touched my weary spirit with His love.

I asked Jesus into my life that very evening
I felt peace no more confusion
As I slowly learned to trust Him
Then I saw my Savior standing
With His arm around me gently
We were standing at the entrance [1]
Of a dark and dreary forest
It was dark and growing darker
But He promised He'd be with me all the way.

It's been a long time since this happened
And my life it changed completely
But there've been times when I've cried out
"My precious Lord why did You leave me"?
But He's always there beside me [2]
Though the path grows cold and lonely

---

[1] *Matthew 7:13-14 "Enter through the narrow gate;…"*
[2] *Deuteronomy 31:8 "… He will be with you. He will not desert you or abandon you."*

And I want to travel with Him
And I want Him close beside me
As I face the coldness of the world today.

And I want to travel with Him
And I want Him close beside me
Won't you take my hand, my friend
As we look to Him together to the end.

Note: Was it a dream or a vision? I do not know. I only know what I experienced was absolutely life changing. I saw myself and Jesus walking together toward a fork in the road. The love I experienced at His side was totally liberating and transformative. We never spoke a word as He walked with me with His hand around my shoulder, but we communicated perfectly and completely. As His love filled my being, like electricity running up and down my body, we stopped at the fork and I knew I would walk the path less traveled.

The Journey

Daughter, it was here where we first started
This journey so very long ago
You came to this place of decision
To choose the way that you would go
The narrow path through the forest
Or the wide gate of the world you knew well[1]
It was here that eternity waited
In the balance was heaven or hell.

Lord, I remember that day of decision
The answer was so very clear
I chose the path less traveled
And your love dispelled all my fear
So pure was the love I encountered
So liberating to my soul
Rivers of pure joy rushing through me
Making clear the way I should go.

---

[1] *Matthew 7:13-14 "Enter through the narrow gate; for the gate is wide and the way is broad that leads to destruction… For the gate is narrow and the way is constricted that leads to life…"*

As we stood side by side My love filled you,
And you knew I'd be with you each day
I smiled through tears and held you closer—
I knew well the price you would pay
For I knew the plans I had for you
And I saw the cross it would take[2]
The storms and fires of refinement—
A pure vessel I was planning to make.[3]

Somehow I knew Lord, I would encounter
Some good days and also the bad
The assurance that You would go with me,
Was the only hope that I really had
Oh, it's true I've not always been faithful
And Your word I've not always obeyed
Many times I failed to focus
On the price that You already paid.[4]

I never promised the way would be easy
Or that you would not struggle through life
True character is built in the darkness
Through heartaches, turmoil and strife
It's my grace and my mercy that lead you—
This I made very clear
For my strength is perfected in weakness[5]
True faith is not based on fear.

At your side I could face all my sorrows

---

[2] *Matthew 16:24 "Then Jesus said to His disciples, 'If anyone wants to come after Me,*
he must deny himself, take up his cross, and follow Me."
[3] *Isaiah 64:8 "But now, Lord, You are our Father; we are the clay, and You our potter,*
and all of us are the work of Your hand."
[4] *Romans 5:8 "But God demonstrates His own love toward us, in that while we were*
still sinners, Christ died for us."
[5] *IICorinthians 12:10 "Therefore I delight in weaknesses…for when I am weak, then*
I am strong."

I could get up each time that I fell
For richness of life in the Spirit
No mortal words could ever tell
For though weeping may last for a nighttime[6]
Joy comes with each morning sun
Your mercies are new every morning
Your faithfulness is toward everyone.

You have come through your journey with triumph
To this place where we first had begun
I have tried you and proved you my daughter
And searched your heart for so very long
The work that I started is completed…
But by no means is it the end
We've come to the place where we started
To do it all over again.

"It's OK Lord" are the words You've heard often—
I'm willing and ready to start
On the road less traveled and lonely—
Just please hold me close to Your heart
For I trust You, my God, you've never failed me
Or left me alone very long
For it's been in my darkest hour
That you faithfully give me a song.

I AM with you My daughter, My sweetness—
your love so true and so pure
You have served Me with your whole heart—
Of My love you can always be sure
For you've been through some good and some bad times
But always remember this
The struggles more than joys in the journey
Are my beloved gifts!

---

[6] *Psalm 30:5 "… Weeping may last for the night, but a shout of joy comes in the morning."*

The Dark Room

This room is a familiar place
She knows the darkness[1] well
Though the things she stumbles over
She cannot always tell
But when at times the light is dim
She can begin to see
Her captors' cruel faces
Oh, who can set her free?

They thrust her in this room that's dark
Mouth gagged so she can't talk
Her hands and feet are bound up tight
She cannot even walk
Her tormentors know her well
They know her weakest parts
She's heard their names so many times,
She knows what's in their hearts.

Insignificance and *Unimportance*
Are two that guard her well
Misunderstanding comes on the scene
To weave his magic spell
Then *Coldness of Heart* comes in again
His iron-cold hands are firm
To grip the heart of compassion
That wants only love to burn.

---

[1] *Isaiah 9:2 "The people who walk in darkness will see a great light; those who live in a dark land, the light will shine on them."*

Unable to talk or express herself
Locked up without a key
Then *Love* Himself steps in the room
And her tormentors flee!
The room lights up and she can see
The room is growing smaller
Or maybe it is she whose size
Is really growing taller.

He speaks to her with words of love
And takes her by the hand
Her captors are all replaced
With *One Who Understands*
This *Liberator* makes her see
With Him she has importance
Proving this one time and again
Developing character through the process.

Now *Faith* steps in to make strong again
The knees that grow so feeble[2]
And *Joy* comes in to hold up the arms
Lifting hands up, she does kneel
Now surely, she is getting free
From the darkness and the gloom
The *Master's* been developing her
In this beloved *Dark Room*.

---

[2] *Hebrews 12:12 "Therefore, strengthen the hands that are weak and the knees that are feeble."*

Laying It Down

Shattered hopes and a future unclear
Lives destroyed by pain and fear
Are there no answers?
Does God not hear?[1]

Strong chains of bondage grip the soul
A vice so strong we can't be whole
Where are the keys?
Does God not know?

Then God replies…
But, indeed, I have seen the pain and I grieve
I have known the affliction but just believe
I have seen the oppression and the chains of fear
For the cries, my precious, have reached my ear
I just want to remind you—for those tears I died
All through the years, faith has been tried
But I've said it before and again I say
Listen to my Spirit, just trust and obey
For from the beginning, the plan was so clear
The purpose established, don't doubt and don't fear!

Give me ears to hear Lord, and eyes to see
All that You have prepared for me[2]
You knew me long before I was born

---

[1] *Isaiah 59:1 "Behold, the Lord's hand is not so short that it cannot save; nor is His ear so dull that it cannot hear."*

[2] *I Corinthians 2:9 "Things which eye has not seen and ear has not heard, and which have not entered the human heart, all that God has prepared for those who love Him."*

You shaped my heart before it was torn
It is courage that I need right now
So, I surrender it all
I am laying it down!

The Rescue

The struggles overwhelm her
Getting buried fast with no relief in sight
The winds whipping her in the desert sand
Scorched and dry she prays with fading faith
And with a growing sense of failure
Will someone come to help…
Someone to care enough…
Someone to come to her rescue?

She waits…and waits…and she waits again
As she waits, hopelessness sets in
The heart becomes weary and "*waited*" down
Singing songs throughout the day
Trying desperately to resurrect faith…
Trying desperately to wake up hope…
Then a phone call comes at an unusual hour
Just to say, "hello."

The call comes just after she cries out to the Lord
Just before she loses all hope
Just before she gives up in total despair
There you were—coming to her wilderness
When all her world seemed dark and dim and oh so dry
Faith restored, peace and joy once again filling her soul
You came bringing light and refreshment…
Washing the hot sand from her battered feet

The incarnate Christ once again
Coming in human form
Who is this coming up out of the wilderness

Leaning on her beloved[1]
Thank you for hearing His heart
I know now that God really cares because you did!
Thank you, Lord, for my friend
Thank you, my friend, for coming to my rescue!

---

[1] *Song of Solomon: "Who is this coming up from the wilderness, leaning on her beloved?"*

Amazing Grace

Peace attends me in my way
Though I face each broken day
As I walk this way, I know
My legs get stronger as I go
The truth is that they are weak
But grace comes lifts me to my feet.[1]

It is the better place for me
A place of sheer dependency
To lean on One so big and strong
He carries me when all goes wrong
I lift my eyes up from this place
And hear the words, "Amazing Grace."

And grace it's been all through the years[2]
Through many dangers, toils and snares
I bow my head to worship Him
Grace comes and holds me firm again
I will get through this mess I know
For where grace takes me, I will go!

---

[1] *Psalm 84:11 "… The Lord gives grace and glory; He withholds no good thing from those who walk with integrity."*
[2] *John 1:16 "For of His fullness we have all received, and grace upon grace."*

Journal Entry: February 7, 2003—Starting a business has been the biggest step of faith of my life. I have all on the altar—all is at stake. The financial pressures are immense! I could feel myself buckling under the pressure. I locked the doors to my new office and went into the conference room where I laid down the burden of it all. The following was birthed as I prayed...

Beyond the Veil

As I walk this earthen sod
I have lived my life for God
As I've taken steps of faith
It's only God—I walk by grace!

Now I lay my burdens down[1]
At His feet, I cast my crown[2]
I will always walk this way
The road of grace is how I came!

When the road becomes obscure
By His grace I can endure
For I will never have to fear
He is my light; the path is clear!

---

[1] *Matthew 11:28-30 "Come to me, all you who labor and are burdened, and I will give you rest."*
[2] *Revelation 4:10-11 "They throw down their crowns before the throne, exclaiming: 'Worthy are you, Lord, to receive glory and honor and power...'"*

Ever pressing for the prize
Distractions come before my eyes
For in this time I cannot fail
The visions are beyond the veil![3]

[3] *Hebrews 10:19 "...since we have confidence to enter the holy place by the blood of Jesus, by a new and living way which He inaugurated for us through the veil..."*

Until Then!

To know you, to love you,
To walk along side of you
This is what I yearn for
This is all I want
You have walked into my heart
And captured my affections
Turning my mourning into dancing
My sorrows into joy.

Thank you, Precious Lord!
You are my *"All in All"*
My refuge and strength
The One whom my soul yearns for
Looks to, welcomes, and embraces
Filling all the cracks and imperfections.

To look to You…to run to You
When rejection comes along
Offering myself as a well-pleasing sacrifice
With mouth full of praise
And heart full of hope
Death to self and all of its cravings
You offer life to all
Who are without faith, hope and love.

Oh yes! Faith, hope and love…these three…
But the greatest is love[1]

---

[1] *I Corinthians 13:13 "So faith, hope, love remain, these three; but the greatest of these is love."*

So teach me, oh Divine One
Teach me your ways
Show me your paths[2]
Keep me on the straight and narrow
The road less traveled
The road of my destiny...*until then!*

[2] *Psalm 25:4 "Make known to me your ways, Lord; teach me your paths."*

On My Knees

Daughter, oh daughter, where have you been?
I've been in the world, Lord, living among men.

Daughter, oh daughter, what found you there?
I found men, women and children
in great need of prayer.

Daughter, oh daughter, what did you there?
I told of Your love and I showed them You care.

Speak, my daughter, how were you received?
By many rejected—I fell to my knees.

I come to your rescue and gather your tears
I shower down grace and remove all your fears
I rise up with power to encourage your heart
I call you to life so from evil depart
I know you and call you—there's a purpose and plan
See here, I've written your name on my hand.[1]

Go forward, my daughter, be confident of this
I cause you to stand with a heart full of bliss
You've come through the storms, the fire and the flood
The evil can't hold you—I have paid with my blood[2]
Draw close to Me, my daughter, my bride
I am your God—I will walk by your side.

---

[1] *Isaiah 49:16 "Behold, I have inscribed you on the palms of My hands…"*
[2] *James 4:7 "Submit therefore to God. But resist the devil, and he will flee from you."*

For mercy and grace, I have called forth this day
And I go before you preparing the way
Go forth, my daughter, and strengthen the others
Encourage the hearts of your sisters and brothers[3]
Reach out to a world with the Word of the Lord
It brings truth and divides like a two-edged sword.

Daughter, my daughter, where have you been?
I've been in the presence of my Master and King.

Daughter, my daughter, what found you there?
I found a great love which displaced all my fears.

Daughter, my daughter, what did you there?
I worshipped my King and offered my prayers.

Daughter, my daughter, how were you received?
I found love overflowing—and fell down on my knees.

---

[3] *Hebrews 3:13 "But encourage one another every day, as long as it is still called 'today' so that none of you will be hardened by the deceitfulness of sin."*

God's Love Cry

"I have come my love
I've heard your heart's cry
And I have come."[1]
His love brings wholeness
To the fragmented places
It is at His side that true love is experienced
It is at His side that one is loved and cared for."

Drink, drink my love—drink deeply—[2]
Drink completely
Drink to your heart's content
Till all that is within you is at peace.

His love comes as a dove
Gently…brings peace to my soul
God's love is deep
A shallow relationship cannot quench
This thirst in my soul
This hunger for intimacy
This drive for completeness.

Drink, drink my love—drink deeply—
Drink completely
Drink to your heart's content
Till all that is within you is satisfied.

---

[1] *Psalm 116:1, 2 "I love the Lord, because He hears my voice and my pleas. Because He has inclined His ear to me, therefore I will call upon Him as long as I live."*

[2] *Song of Solomon 5:1 "I have come into my garden, my sister, my bride;… Eat, friends; drink and drink deeply, lovers."*

Walk with Me my love
Lie down and rest
And let the world move on
Explore all that is in your reach
Probe into the secret places…
The hidden places
Of your soul and spirit."

Drink, drink my love—drink deeply—
Drink completely
Drink to your heart's content
Till all that is within you is satisfied

For within every soul
There is a key within reach
The door opens
You are free to discover His love
"You are my joy and my delight
Let your soul drink and be satisfied
Let your heart dream and be refreshed."

Drink, drink my love—drink deeply—
Drink completely
Drink to your heart's content
Till all that is within you is satisfied.

Journal Entry: July 13, 2019 At a women's conference in Buffalo, I sat at the table with Dr. Sandra Cobham, Pastor at Dominion Life Christian Center in Niagara Falls, NY. She touched my heart as I was drawn by the depth of her spirit.

After we connected so deeply, we realized that this truly was a divine appointment. You see, she was originally seated at another table, and at the last minute, Pastor Sandra moved to my table. To God be the glory! It was an encouraging time, and we were both grateful for this beautiful connection!

The Woman of God

A tribute to the army of courageous women who impact our world!

Woman of purpose and power
The woman is birthing this very hour
Standing so strong and serene
Yielded to Him who is so Supreme

A quiet strength mighty and strong
Moves in VICTORY—she cannot go wrong
Breaking limitations off of you and of me
God has called her to set women free

Free to be so strong and serene
On the favor of God, they learn how to lean
A woman of Character
There is no doubt
She knows how to listen
And knows to reach out

Trustworthy
Kind
Follows Him
Obeys
Tearing down strongholds
From darkness they're saved

To go beyond from the places she's been
So much favor and grace as she walks close to Him
Rescuing those who cry out from this sod
So much more to come—from this Woman of God!!

The Beatitudes[1]

A stranger came knocking upon my heart's door one day
How could I open with such disarray!
But His voice it was calling—He was calling my name[2]
I'd never felt such longing so in spite of my shame,
I opened the door and He walked right in
He brought peace and gave me a reason to live
For never had I encountered such love
He wiped away tears, gave me peace from above
This love stepped in and made everything new[3]
The old passed away now I have a new view.

It was the power of a love so simple and pure
So full and redeeming, gave me steps that were sure
This stranger has truly become my best friend
He promised to stay—of His love there's no end
For this road is dreary at times and so bleak
But the earth He has promised to those who are meek
To those who are hungry and thirsting for more
He will satisfy and fill—of this I am sure.

This heart that's been blessed and made pure by His hand
Has seen God at work and can now understand
Sons of God He calls those who make peace
And to those who show mercy, it's mercy they receive

---

[1] *Matthew 5:1-12 "Now when Jesus saw the crowds, He went up on the mountain;… And he opened His mouth and began to teach them…"*

[2] *Song of Solomon 5:2 "…a voice! My beloved was knocking: 'Open to me, my sister, my darling, my dove, my perfect one!"*

[3] *IICorinthians 5:17 "Therefore if anyone is in Christ, this person is a new creation; the old things passed away; behold, new things have come."*

Rejoice and be glad when people insult you
And say all manner of evil against you
For your reward in heaven is great
This is a promise to anticipate.

When mourning and weeping, He comforts my soul
Gives beauty for ashes and now I'm made whole
So long ago I first opened the door
He blesses and blesses each day more and more.
Supreme blessedness, peace, and grace has replaced
This totally broken and messed up place!
For His ways and His thoughts are different you see
Than the ways of the world and its tendencies.

These are the things I've learned and seen in my life
As I've walked with God's Word as my guiding light
You'll see God if you have a heart that is pure
To see as God sees will help you endure
To those who are humble and poor in spirit
It is heaven's kingdom that they stand to inherit
This is God's way and I've always confessed
I am blessed, I am blessed, I am blessed, I am blessed!

Journal Entry: January 30, 1984—I dreamt I came into a room where the women from church were praying. There was music playing and some were on their beds sleeping and some were on the floor praying. I heard the words of a song Jesus was singing to Mary. I was inspired to write this poem.

My First Love[1]

Oh Mary, my Mary, why do you weep?
You've been forgiven, now stand to your feet
For such great love you have in your heart
Much you've been forgiven, much love you impart
Your love shows so much gratitude to Me
Your faith has saved you, go live in peace
Go tell the people of all I have done
For you have been touched by God's only Son
But as you go tell the others, come back to this place
And remember this time that we talked face-to-face.

As for me, same as Mary, much has been forgiven
My life is a story of all He has given
But too often with life I get carried away
And forget to come back day after day
To the place at His feet where with thankfulness I cried
When I realized it was for me that He died
I will remember His love when my heart He did fill
When I stood at His side and was quiet and still
For He is my first love—how I love to remember this place
When He gave me new life and we talked face-to-face.

---

[1]   *Luke 7:37-50 "…there was a woman in the city who was a sinner;…her sins, which are many, have been forgiven, for she loved much; but the one who is forgiven little, loves little…"*

The Transforming Power of God

Oh, transforming power of God
Transcending all of my human frailties and inabilities
Ah yes! Now I understand
It is by this door that you enter in
You strengthen frail humanity
And enter through the door of our weak hearts

The prideful boast, "We are not weak!"
The rich boast, "We have no need!"
Deceived they be that cannot see
We are wretched and poor—
At our worst, we are despicable
At our best—tolerable
At our point of need—transformable![1]

For when we are weak, then we are strong[2]
Hungering and thirsting, we are fed
Weakened by the storms of life
We are made whole
By the transforming power of God!

---

[1] *Romans 12:2 "…be transformed by the renewing of your mind…"*
[2] *II Corinthians 12:10 "Therefore I delight in weaknesses, in insults, in distresses, in persecutions, in difficulties, in behalf of Christ; for when I am weak, then I am strong."*

The Standard

The Auditor came and found my life lacking
Non-conformances abounding and so much more!
How could I start to make all things right?
How would I tackle this chore?

Then He pointed me to *The Standard*
So I studied and studied and learned how to give
It was all about life and how to embrace it
Putting His Word into practice, it taught me to live

Now I look at my life and I am certainly blessed
He's definitely *Added Value* to me
All is in order and I am at rest
From burdens and hassles I'm free

I'm free 'cause I call my *Consultant*
It's His counsel I seek day and night
I do all He tells me to do
For He teaches me only what's right[1]

And someday when this life is ended
And the race is finished and run
I will hear the words from *The Standard*
Well done! My good and faithful one![2]

---

[1] *John 14:26: "But the Helper, the Holy Spirit whom the Father will send in My name, He will teach you all things…"*

[2] *Matthew 25:23 "His master said to him, 'Well done, good and faithful slave. You were faithful with a few things, I will put you in charge of many things; enter the joy of your master.'"*

Then I'll have my final approval
I will enter into my rest
For I looked to Jesus, *The Standard*
It is written He gave us His very best!

Part Three

Let Go of Control...
Hold On To Your
MARRIAGE

Marriage Struggles

In 1968 Russ and I met in a bar. We kept on connecting in bars—that's what we and our friends did—the drinking age was 18. We loved the bar scene—the drinking, the dancing, the bands, the music. It was "fun." In 1969, we were married. We believed with all of our hearts that we would live "happily ever after" and that the pain of our childhood years was behind us.

In 1970, our first son was born and after Russ completed his military duty, we finally were able to start our new lives together with our four-month-old baby. What I didn't realize is that our lives would be bombarded by the ravages of alcohol addiction.

What we experienced in the first seven years of our marriage was the unspeakable heartache and strife of alcohol addiction which led to much emotional and physical abuse. His father, an alcoholic, his mother busy with eight children didn't have time to give a lot of attention to her seventh child. He learned at a young age to build walls around his sensitive, caring heart. Then at the age of 12, he realized that he could numb his pain with alcohol.

Our lives were unraveling at a fast pace until the time I experienced a life-changing spiritual encounter with Jesus Christ. The love and peace this brought into my life was nothing short of a miracle.

For the next seven years, Russ continued to drink but God's love and peace remained. Russ's continued use of alcohol could not take my new-found peace away from me.

Then, in 1980, Russ too surrendered his life to Jesus and the bar scene changed to the church scene where we became very involved with a beautiful community of believers.

We were devoted parents encouraging and supporting our three sons who have grown to be responsible adults and faithful fathers and husbands.

It was difficult as we entered into our season of being "empty-nesters." Now it was just the two of us with no distractions. As the years passed, I still struggled with the empty feeling of our marriage. Something was terribly wrong but I could not identify or understand fully what I was dealing with. I knew it had to do with his inability to show his emotions.

Slowly through the years, alcohol repeatedly popped up its ugly head. In 2016, I left Russ for a year. With two weeks until the divorce was finalized, something broke in Russ. He cried out in prayer one night. In fact, he shouted so loud, he thought he would wake up the neighbors. The walls that Russ had built since a child, finally crumbled and fell.

We began to slowly reunite. Our healing path led us to the work of psychologist Dr. Doug Weiss. "Intimacy Anorexia" is a term that he coined that had to do with issues related to emotional or physical intimacy which can have a major impact on a relationship. We finally had the key to understand and bring healing and wholeness into our union.

Today we are a testimony of God's keeping power. In 2019, we celebrated 50 years of marriage. We experienced God make something beautiful and good out of it all. There is not a day that goes by that we don't thank God for getting our lives on track.

These poems will give a glimpse into the heartache and brokenness of a woman who for years experienced the ravages and pain of a husband with an addiction to alcohol. Over and over again, it would pop up its ugly head. Just when we seemed to be on the other side of it, we would go around and around again and again.

The addiction, of course, is not the problem but it just points to a much deeper problem within. Through it all, we have learned much about each other as we have leaned heavily on our God's strong arm. Slowly, we emerged out of the rubble of brokenness and into a greater understanding of life.

A Marriage and Its Prisoners

Where are the books that should have been written
The songs that could have been sung
Of a love so rich and fulfilling
The love we both yearned for so long

But deep in my prison I'm hiding
A slave of sadness and grief
My feelings of little importance
Of these things we never could speak

You never ask, "What is the matter?"
"Can we talk, can I help you my sweets?"
It would have made all the difference
But you could show no intimacy

So I live here within my prison
When my heart just yearns to be free
Free from these walls of confinement
Free to love with all that's within me

Someday I'll escape from this prison
Of loneliness, sadness and grief
I'll unlock the door to your prison
But just now I can't find the key

For you've been so long in your prison
A little boy too afraid to come out
A safe place it's been in your prison
Not feeling the pain in your heart

As a child you ran to this safe place
Just ignore what was happening outside
And you were safe in your room of denial
No pain was lurking about

Someday when you emerge from your prison
You'll be a man happy and free
You'll face the neglect of your childhood
And you'll have the key to come loosen me!

Won't! Can't! Never!

Go ahead ignore the issues,
Hide your head in the sand again
Go ahead patch the wall
I won't try to break it down again since
I won't see you anymore! I won't care!

So many times with a chisel, a hammer, a crane
But no more—there's no more trying again
So many times I tried to break down that wall…
I promise I can't try again because
I can't see you anymore! I can't care!

Just when I thought I was getting somewhere
I'd find the wall mended again
Just when I for the "millionth" time said, "One last time…"
I never found my strength again, now…
I'll never see you anymore! I'll never care!

You've made it clear so go ahead live your life
But it will be without me
You've made it clear you like the wall
You won't change and that's OK since
You won't see me anymore! You won't care!

You've drawn the line—
I will finally respect your wishes
You've drawn the line—
You can't go where we need to go, because
You can't see me anymore! You can't care!

You could have helped to break down the wall
Just a bit at a time
You could have at least allowed the cracks and the holes
That I worked so hard on but, now
You'll never see me anymore! You'll never care!

48 years—it's been long enough
Goodbye!

Yoyo

She keeps working
Optimistic and bright
She keeps moving
But feeling hampered
So weighted down
Very heavy
Very burdened
Can't get past the feelings

What is this thing
That slows her down?
That always stops her cold?
That draws life out?
Slowly, succinctly, purposefully
Till life is gone
Can't continue
Feels lost and out of touch

Then she stops
Long enough to realize
She's living with a dead man
Unable to talk
Unable to dream
Unable to move beyond
Unable to take the lead
Or at least walk beside her

Feels stuck
Just stuck
What next?

Where next?
How next?
Not again!
Up and down
Like a yoyo![1]

---

[1] *When life feels like a yoyo, no matter the ups or the downs know that you'll always end up in the hands of Almighty God." (Victoria Osteen)*

82 | ANTONINA CAPRINO BELL

The Merry-Go-Round

Round and round and round she goes
Where she stops is a VERY familiar place
She gets stuck in a rut that's as deep as a grave
It traps her and swallows her up
Each time she finds it more difficult to get out
Somehow she manages—somehow she's on top again
But not without the wounds of battle
Battle against the forces that keep her struggling
How could he be so blind? She wonders
Does he not understand
Even though he's heard it 45,000 times?
Two simple words, "Let's talk."
Is that so hard to say?
His tongue is tied always when it comes to her
45,000 words she's spoken
And him? No words—no words are ever there
What is the answer to her dilemma?
When she needs a shelter
When she needs a friend
Where does she go?
Who does she run to?
She runs to the *The* Rock—she runs to her Savior
She questions. When? How Long? Why?
She tries to accept what she cannot change and thinks,
"I'll never go this way again."
No matter what road she chooses though,
It always ends up making a big circle back to the same place
Back to the grave that gets her stuck
Keeps her struggling to get out
Is there no getting away?

Is there no hope?
She just keeps on accepting
Keeps on trying again and again
She keeps on believing
She just keeps on going round and round
Till death do them part...

Deciding to leave my husband after 47 years turned out to be the most painful decision I had ever made. It tore me in pieces to have to give up all I had worked so hard for. It was certainly a death experience. The grief was overwhelming.

If I had lost my husband in a physical death, it would have been easier—at least there would have been many to comfort me. The hardest part was the isolation, separation and judgment I felt from those around me.

Every morning I would start my day by spending time in prayer and lots of crying. One day I had ONLY used 12 tissues and I felt that it was a good start of my day feeling that I was coming out of my grief!

In the Shadows…

Finding herself at a very different place
Never been here but always been here
In all her getting she wants understanding
To her God she must be true
Hanging out under the shadows
Seeking, wanting she knows not who
She knows not what

In this unclear place she searches for meaning
For relevance, for connections
Finding none, she stumbles
"Lord, don't let me fall," she prays
She is held close so close that she can feel His heartbeat
She needs God's grace so very much
Desperately, she reaches…she grasps…

She believes…she foolishly believes
So wounded…so limited…so isolated

Must she always be at this place? She questions
Must she always have to endure the pain…
the rejection…the loss?
What is the answer, she wonders
What is her life all about?
She gave, she gave, and she gave
And she hungered for more—oh how she hungered
But there was no one there
No one to encourage, no one to cheer her on
No one faithful to protect her

Misunderstood, always misunderstood
Others don't know nor do they try to know her
Finds herself deserted by her best friend
In her hour of need, in her time of testing
She runs, she flees, she hides
And she lingers…in the shadows…

Journal Entry: July 1984—With my husband and two young sons by my side, everything looked wonderful on the outside. There we were a young family—father, mother and children—but inside, my heart was breaking. We were spending the afternoon at the zoo and there in front of us sat an eagle perched in a cage made of thick steel bars.

As I stood before this wonderful creature behind those horrible bars, I remembered the scene from the night before of my intoxicated husband crawling into our dining room where he passed out just at the foot of the stairs. There he slept all night. As I remembered that scene, my heart was breaking because I knew this was not how God intended the man or the eagle should live. Both were captive and unable to rise to the splendor of their potential and purpose." It was here that "The Eagle Song" was birthed.

The Eagle Song

The eagle was inside his cage
Sitting ever so still
He peered through eyes that seemed to say,
Don't look at me this is not God's will.
I can fly you see, so high in the sky
If you saw me you'd realize
That God made me far superior
I am a mighty bird!

Flying, soaring, ever so high
I am a captive here
But I must get out and fly!
Flying, soaring, so high in the sky
That is where I must be
Won't you set me free!

My mind went to another cage
The cage made by man
The broken homes and empty lives
This was not God's plan
You can fly, you see, so high in the sky
If you knew Him, you'd realize
Far superior did God make man
You can be born again!

They that wait upon the Lord[1]
They shall-they shall renew their strength
They shall mount up with wings as eagles
They shall run and not be weary
They shall walk and not faint
Teach me Lord, teach me Lord
Teach me to wait!

Flying, soaring, ever so high
God gave me wings as eagles
To fly high in sky
Far above my problems
In peace and harmony
Looking to Jesus Christ
He came to set men free!

---

[1] *Isaiah 40:31 "Yet those who wait for the Lord will gain new strength; they will
mount up with wings like eagles, they will run and not get tired, they will walk and
not become weary.*

Journal Entry: June 21, 2017—After 48 years of marriage, not a word from the man I gave my all to. As if we never existed. No thought of me at all. Just nothing. I am so broken, feeling so lost and so unloved. And that's Not OK.

Down For the Count...

Life as black as midnight
Love as cold as ice
Darkness creeping in
Abandoned and disillusioned
No worth, no value
Failures, disappointments

She gave and gave
Until nothing was left
Just a shadow of what or who
Could have been

All but forgotten
Within a pit of pain
Looking, hoping, being
Lost and alone with no one coming
No hope for tomorrow
Forsaken, rejected, abandoned—Oh so abandoned!

She gave and gave
Until nothing was left
Just a shadow of what or who
Could have been

Never looked after
Never cherished or adored
No one knows, no one cares
Down flat for the count
Not her first time down, but this time…
She may never rise again…

The Storms[1]

Broken but not shattered
Wounded but still whole
The peace still flows like a mighty river
I run to the rock that is higher than I
I stand even though the waves roll over me
Feels like I'm drowning but I stand secure

The fire's hot but I pray the dance is still in me
I pray that something will come out of this furnace[2]
This hell of loneliness, despair, deep sorrow
Sorrow for a lifetime of shattered dreams
A lifetime of wondering, "Who am I?"
"Why am I here?" "For what purpose do I exist?"

The answers will come on the wings of a new day
The answers will come—I know they will
They shall rest gentle on my mind
Soft in my spirit—a tried spirit
For the spirit of a woman when coupled with God's Spirit
Is strong—can stand the testing, the trials

Oh Creator of the universe, come rise up within me
Through it all, this marriage can be healed and whole
Take me to the place of weening
The place of the calm after the storm
Be filled, oh my soul—be filled with good things
Rest again in His peace after the storms

---

[1] Matthew 7:24-27 "… And the rain fell and the floods came, and the winds blew and
   slammed against that house, and yet it did not fall, for it had been founded on the rock…"
[2] Daniel 3:13-27 "…walking about in the middle of the fire unharmed…"

Journal Entry: March 8, 2002

It's been so very discouraging. More than once, I've been at the point of hopelessness. As soon as I would surrender my dreams and ambitions and give up, a new hope would seem to well up inside of me. I would cry out to the Lord when everything seemed to be weighing heavily on my shoulders. I would have to lay down my vision one more time—be willing to let go.

Just as I am willing to give it up, something happens that gives me the most profound sense that I need to keep moving forward and not drop my anchor nor embrace hopelessness. A deep peace settles in on me and I am once again graced with so much favor. A greater sense of destiny is keeping me afloat.

Keep On Moving!

One thing she's learned is that she cannot accept defeat
She must keep on sailing—no matter what
She needs to keep believing
and moving forward
Sometimes it feels as though
she will surely go down
But she keeps on moving
As if she is scaling a giant cliff
She reaches for just one more hold
for her hand or foot
And suddenly it's there—
Out of darkness, it reveals itself
And she moves just a little bit closer to her destiny—
to her vision

It's more than about who she is
or what she needs
But it's as though she is being moved and
shaped for a higher purpose
It's hard to explain but she sees it
It's often vague and sometimes without form
Yet it is clear deep down inside

As time passes, more clarity comes
But only as she keeps on sailing—
Keeps on moving
Never daunted by the unsettling waves
Or the unclear path
Keeps casting her bread upon the waters [1]
Knowing it will return after many days
She just keeps on casting—keeps on giving

The ocean is deep and wide and forever
And that is the love she holds for God and others
That keeps her moving
Reflecting the deep love of God
That is able to cut through the blackness
And the sea of endless faces crying out
Hands always reaching for a lifeline
So she keeps on giving[2]
Keeps on offering hope for the hopeless
And she won't stop
She won't drop her anchor
She just keeps on moving

---

[1] *Ecclesiastes 11:1 "Cast your bread on the surface of the waters, for you will find it after many days."*
[2] *Acts 20:35 "In everything I showed you that by working hard in this way you must help the weak and remember the words of the Lord Jesus, that He Himself said 'It is more blessed to give than to receive.'"*

Empty Nest

Our family
is
grown
and gone
and so
too
is gone
Our reason
to be together
since we never
had a relationship
to
begin
with
I guess
we're
finished…
and…
it's time to
move on!

Defeated? NOT!

My knees are bleeding—I've prayed too long
My spirit is bruised—I've hoped too hard
My legs are weak—I've stood too long
My hands are sore—I've worked too hard
My heart is broken
The wick is flickering
The flame has died
But… It is not the end—
It is just a new beginning!

More Than a Hand

A Little girl stood beside her father in church
Her little hands entwined around his
She would lean on that hand so big and so strong
She knew only comfort and she knew only bliss

What strength she found there at his side
Receiving love and help with no end
She's known well this hand of provision and care
Her protector, her daddy, her friend

On his other side stood a woman serene
His friend, his beauty, his bride
Hands clasped together, they'd look at each other
With love, passion and pride

We have a Heavenly Father
Who stands with us side by side
We can know his hand of provision
Or we can know His heart for His bride

I have known His hand of provision
I have leaned hard on his hand so strong
Then I grew up and put away childish things[1]
At His side is where I belong

---

[1] *I Corinthians 13:11, 12 "… I put away childish things. For now we see in a mirror dimly, but then face to face…"*

Face to face is how I must know Him
Looking full in His wonderful eyes
I worship this One I call Jesus
He's my Husband, my Master, my prize!

When? How?

When did I stop calling you "hon"?
Was it after all the nights you were late coming home?
Or the times you came home not able to walk straight?
When? When did it happen?
When did my heart get so hard and my voice so cold?

How did the life go out of my eyes?
Eyes that once danced at the sight of you—
How did my heart change?
It once beat faster at the sound of your voice
How did it happen?

When did hope slip out of my hands?
Love—dashed to pieces—torn from my heart?
When did I stop talking? Stop laughing? Stop hoping?
It's time for change, we both know
Change? Change of attitude—change of heart

We stand at a threshold of a new tomorrow
Forgetting those things that are behind, we look ahead
To a new future filled with forgiveness and tenderness
When did I start calling you "sweetheart"?
How did I start loving you again?

To My Man

I am woman
Watch me stand
But I need you to hold my hand
I need you to reach out
To hold me
To touch me
Intimately...lovingly...
I am the wife of your youth[1]
Take care of me
I'm fragile in many areas
Lacking...
So often lacking
So often left with wanting more
Needing more of you...
Needing to feel special to you
To be important to you
To be romanced by you.

---

[1] *Malachi 2:14 "... Be careful then about your spirit, and see that none of you deal treacherously against the wife of your youth."*
Isaiah 54:6 "For the Lord has called you, like a wife forsaken and grieved in spirit, even like a wife of one's youth when she is rejected, says your God."

My Inspiration

Reaching...
Touching...
Holding...
Building...
Lines of communication...
Connecting...
Joining...
Till two are one and one is two
Separate...
Yet together...
Joined...
Yet still undone...
Breathing...
Hoping...
Wanting...
Yearning for more of you!
You inspire me!

Passion, My Old Friend

Passion, how did you capture her heart old friend?
How did you walk into this place again?
What was it you said that sparked a dying ember?
Embers in the fire of life that once burned bright

Passions that yearned for the deep
That almost drowned this one who could not swim alone
She cried out many times but there was never an answer
Ear was not given and no progress was made

The soil was hard and had never been softened
Too hard for this frail one—
Now on the other side of summer
Summer—with lovers strolling through the park

Hand-in-hand, arm-in-arm
Sailboats linger—content on the still waters
Where nights are peaceful and cool
The moon casts its light of lovers in the night

Once upon a time she thought herself strong
But her strength waned and time passed
And passion retreated through time's passing
She busied her life with so much

Involved in so many noble works
For so long and so many times one left unsatisfied
For so long and so many times one left yearning
Yearning for what? Yearning for who?

Passion has renewed many a soul in this world
A world that has almost lost its poetry
In a world that has almost lost its song—
Its passion—its life

So long had she desired… So long…
How weary the journey
So well trained to stifle
So well trained to be content

Content to say goodbye to her old friend
For she is older yet now realizes
That the mind, unlike the body, never changes
The soul of the woman never dies

Being cherished never loses its charm
And romance never loses its magic
Magic that transforms no matter what age
Transcending…erasing the harsh lines of time!

To My Husband

You are my completion—
My other half that I searched for all of my life
Through the years of distance and loneliness
God himself had to step in
And that is what has kept me all these years

Now I feel as though we have been connected—
Connected for a purpose much bigger than you and me
Yet you and I are at the center—together, inseparable—
Destined from the foundations of the world
To be a part of each other—one with each other

I realize more than ever
That you are my completion and I am yours
We are each other's fulfillment—
Each other's reason for living—for breathing—
As if our breaths are one, our heartbeats in sync

You a part of me and I am a part of you
Nothing else can make sense—
Nothing else has true meaning
Living and working side-by-side—
Hand-in-hand

One thing I know, sweetheart,
I cannot live a day without the thoughts of you
I cannot make sense of tomorrow without you
I understand yesterday and tomorrow better
Because you are in my today

As far as the east is from the west,
We've been removed from our past
As close as the sky touches the ocean
When it connects with the horizon
So close are my thoughts to you

Your love has penetrated my soul and spirit
So that you are ever-living in me
Pulsing with my heart's beat—
Flowing through me as wine flows into the cup
Let it fill you to overflowing!!

I love you!

Golden Anniversary
1969-2019

We are so grateful for the time when we reaffirmed our love and commitment to each other in the presence of our family and friends. We understand more deeply that the agape love of God is not dependent on what we do or don't do. God's love is always there steady and constant.

We were so messed up when we first began our lives together but we have experienced God make something beautiful and good out of it all. There is not a day that goes by that we don't thank God for getting our lives on track.

Our three sons are the fruit of our union. It has given us so much joy to see the men they have become. Parenting has been so rewarding and we are forever grateful. To see our sons in action as brothers, friends, workers, husbands, fathers has been a joy and a privilege.

September 27, 2019—50 years later—we celebrated our lives together and it was to God we dedicated that night!

Part Four

Let Go and Loosely...
Hold On To Your
FAMILY

*Dedicated to my three sons who will always be at
the center of my heart forever and always!*

Walk In Your Destiny

I am praying for you oh beloved ones
That peace will attend your way
That things will go well with you
That your way would be prosperous and blessed
In all that you put your hand to do.[1]

Know that you are loved and cared for
I'm in your balcony cheering you on!
Feel the pure energy of love as you sleep
And when you awaken
Let that love carry you through your day.

Let it fill up your senses with a new realization
Of power and ability beyond yourself
Be at peace with yourself and the world around you[2]
Allow love to carry you to new places—
To new heights of fulfillment.

Love simply and purely—love with no strings attached[3]

---

[1] *Psalm 1:3 "… And in whatever he does, he prospers*
[2] *Phillipians 4:6-7 "Do not be anxious about anything, but in everything by prayer
and pleading with thanksgiving let your requests be made known to God. And the
peace of God, which surpasses all comprehension, will guard your hearts and minds
in Christ Jesus.*
[3] *Luke 6:27, 28 "But I say to you who hear, love your enemies, do good to those who
hate you, bless those who curse you, pray for those who are abusive to you."*

With no boundaries—no expectations
A supernatural love that transcends space and time
A love that comes from the omnipotent heart of God
Whose breath and hand formed all we see—all we are.

Live life to the fullest oh precious one
Squeeze every ounce of hope out of every situation
Tap into the river of life
Even though the current overwhelms at times
Give yourself to complete abandonment.

Let that river wash away any rough edges
Till all is renewed and refreshed.
With your gaze turned upward, follow your heart
The inner sense that keeps you in peace
An intense sense of destiny.

Never forget the simple things of life—
Pleasures that are free for the taking—
A smile from a child…
People strolling in the midst of the rushing crowds…
Take time to observe—take time to be.

Never neglect the hand and heart of a child
Or the wisdom of the aged
Or the shouts and whispers of nature
For it is here that true life is discovered
Pour yourself into what you believe.

Hold your hands open and upright
For what you hold is for a season of time
Never clutch things tightly to your bosom
You cannot keep what you do not own
You do not own what you cannot keep.

Let today's joys and disappointments shape you
Never lust after wealth
But keep on casting your bread upon the sea of life
For soon it will return to you on every wave[4]
And overtake you in blessings.

Attend to the needs of others
Life is more than you see or know
Experience the peace that guides your steps
Let today's joys and disappointments shape you
And show you the path you are destined to take.
Pursue life…pursue love…pursue peace…
Walk in your destiny!

---

[4] *Ecclesiastes 11:1 "Cast your bread on the surface of the waters, for you will find it after many days*

A Godly Heritage[1]

A Godly heritage, a good inheritance
Put all of the wealth I have accumulated
From a life of service to You, Lord
Into the accounts of each of my children
And my children's children

Treasures more precious than silver
Riches more costly than gold
These cannot be measured on paper
But summed up by a life here on earth
Bringing love to the unlovely
Hope for the despairing
Caring birthed from worship and praise

Out of my lack, may they have plenty
Out of my pain, may they know grace
Out of my struggles, may they have peace
Out of their peace and harmony
May they connect to the God of all LIFE.
This is my prayer of blessing for my children…

---

[1]   *Proverbs 20:7 "A righteous person who walks in his integrity how blessed are his sons after him.*

Gift of Love[1]

The family's love is such a gift
It makes all things new
Allows the heart to grow and thrive
Love is the electricity
That keeps everything ticking
It flows smoothly through the soul
Transforms life to more than mere existence
It undergirds and supports from a firm foundation

It is a love that brings security and a sense of belonging
When it is lacking, the door opens to much dysfunction
Filling the empty spaces with that which brings bondage
But it's love that can free and connect hearts
Whether that family is through our bloodline
Or created by meaningful communities,
We all crave to be connected to others
And we are blessed with this gift called "Love."[2]

---

[1] *I Corinthians 13:4 "Love is patient, love is kind, it is not jealous; love does not brag, it is not arrogant.*

[2] *I Corinthians 13:13 "But now faith, hope and love remain, these three; but the greatest of these is love."*

Journal Entry: March 22, 1998 My brother, Tony's birthday.
Remembering the pain of our childhood, it hurt to think about the abuse
we went through as children with a father and mother who were out of
control. We rebelled big time in our teen years. Tony was so talented and
had such a caring and sensitive heart and so full of life. As a birthday
gift, I had a picture framed of a little boy and his dog who were huddled
in the corner. The little boy reminded me of my precious brother. This
poem was a result of that picture.

The Corner

Through the years, you've wondered
Just who would stand with you
In that lonely place—the corner
Just pain and hurt you knew

You had no dog to cuddle
Or one to see you through
You only had the pain and hurt
But none to comfort you

Although it's taken many years
I just want you to know
That I am in your corner
And I will NEVER go!

Tony, My Trusted Friend and Brother

The one true joy in life is the love of a brother
He is a safe place—a secure place
A trusted and reliable friend
One with whom to share my heart
One who is totally and completely dedicated
He to me and I to him

With so much turmoil in our home
We were never close growing up
But through the years you have shown
That you are my trusted friend

There was a time that we were not close
Now, for over thirty years, we've deeply connected
You have had such a listening and understanding heart
You've taught me much about myself
Thank you for being at the center
Of my heart and soul—I love you!

The Gift

As I looked around my living room this morning
Admiring the pictures, and the lush, green plants
The special gifts you have given—
I realized that you, my brother,
Have placed beauty all around me
Not only in my home but you've decorated my life!

You have brought understanding
It stands solid beneath me
There are boundaries created
They kept me safe and secure
The love you brought has been the substance
It is in my heart—filling all of the empty places

Thank you!
For this gift of love
It is the treasure of today
And my hope for tomorrow
It is my inheritance to pass on to others
And the tie that binds me to you—
Forever and always!

Journal Entry: July 19, 1996

Grandson, Tyler—A very special baby came into this world on this date. A special baby because he is my first-born grandson. My life's been blessed to have three sons, and now, this precious gift of a grandson. He gives me so much joy and love. I call him "Little Foot."

I was so happy to hold this little precious baby that day at the hospital. My son asked me, "How does it feel to be a grandmother?" I responded, "I'll let you know when he's running into my arms."

Then one day I'll never forget when this little toddler came to my house for a sleep-over carrying his little "Going to Grandma's" overnight bag running down the hall into my arms and I swung him around and we hugged.

Journal Entry: July 19, 1999

"As I drove away from this little face crying in the window, I cried too. For nothing is so precious as to feel wanted and loved. Nothing is as pure as the love of a child. My precious Tyler will be moving soon; thankfully, only four hours away. There will be a great void in this grandmother's heart for her special little boy!

So Glad There's You!

Little face crying in the window
Do you know you're my delight!
Nothing more I'd like to do
Than take you in my arms each night

Blowing kisses from the window
Eyes so red and face so sad
Special weekend I will treasure
Filling in for mom and dad

Grandma will forever love you
Always here to help and cheer
Arms and heart are always open
Quick to put out every fear!

I do remember so long ago
When my family had just begun
A face like yours so sweet and pure
You call him "dad"—I call him "son"

Oh, how the years have swiftly passed
Where did they go? I thought they'd last
But things have changed and sons have too
That's why I'm so glad there's YOU!

In loving tribute to
Peyton Rene Bell, Precious Infant Granddaughter
July 12, 1998

A Flower

July 15, 1998

A little flower was planted today
Peyton Rene Bell
Too precious to hold here on earth
She lay lifeless and still in my arms
A blossom not able to bloom
Drawing hearts together
To comfort through the pain
A flower too beautiful for words

Though denied life, her memory lingers
And so linger the thoughts of what will not be
No crying to be heard nor laughter
No priceless moments of bonding and love
No excitement and no times of exploring
This world filled with awe and wonder
When seen through the eyes of a child
This curious world filled with the beauty of roses
And the sting of thorns!

Life is fragile and so infinitely precious
Treasure the moments and take nothing for granted

Look through the eye of a single day
We cannot look through to tomorrow
Life is wrapped up in trials and tears
But keep on rejoicing, live life to the fullest
Make every day count with those who are near
And remember to treasure each flower!

To my Granddaughter, Adrianna. You have grown to be such an amazing young woman with such a compassionate heart. I will always treasure the memories of our times together. Thank you for bringing so much fun and laughter into my life. One memorable night was around the campfire when you were just four. You wanted me to walk to the house with you and I told you it was too dark to see. I can still feel your little hand in mine and I can hear you so clearly say, "Grandma, I Will Be Your Eyes." You are not only my eyes but you are my heart my Princess!!

I Will Be Your Eyes

The seasons come, the season go
A new life—a new generation[1]
And with each passing day, life goes on
Carried on by new faces—new hearts.

How precious is that little hand in mine
Night covered in darkness
Campfire glowing bright
"Can you walk with me in the dark, grandma?"
"It's much too dark—it's hard to see child."

"That's OK, Grandma. I will be your eyes."
"Yes, my Princess, you will be my eyes."
Lead on my child and hold my hand
My grasp is sure—my hands are secure.

---

[1] *Psalm 78:6-7 "So that the generation to come would know, the children yet to be born, that they would arise and tell them to their children, so that they would put their confidence in God and not forget the works of God,..."*

You can walk in the paths that I have trodden
Continue my journey, daughter
I pass the baton on to you
Take up where I leave off
Be my eyes—see through eyes of faith.

These eyes behold the good in this world
Never lose sight of it
These eyes behold the suffering
Remember always to pray.

The seasons come, the seasons go
One new life—one new generation
And with each passing day, life goes on
Carried on by a new face—a new heart.
Be my eyes, my Princess!

(A letter from Adrianna—March 2017)

Dear Grandma,

No amount of words could ever describe the eternal love and gratitude I have for you and everything you have done for me. Having your love and support means the world to me. I am forever grateful to have you as my grandma.

Even though I vaguely remember the night at my house when I told you I would "be your eyes," I remember you telling me about it. But throughout my life it has been you that are my eyes and the Lord that has been yours. I truly aspire to live such a fulfilling life that I have watched from your life as I have grown up.

Also I would be lucky to encounter a fraction of the blessings that you have been led to. From sitting at the counter at the house on Forest Avenue listening to you talk about your experiences in Honduras and reading the Bible to hearing about your time in Africa, I can't even begin to fathom the amazing opportunities that have come your way.

I admire your dedication, compassion, and integrity that you have not only shown me, but everyone and everything in your life.

Forever and always,
Adrianna

To My Grandson, Drake! Thanks for the memories of the times we have shared together. Your many talents and abilities shine through in all you do. At Mission Meadows camp you heard a Christian hip-hop artist, Lecrae for the first time and you called and excitedly told me about him. You had such a beautiful hunger and enthusiasm for God. Never lose that! It is your key to life!

Famous Sweaty T-Shirt

What special memories! One in particular was taking a trip with Drake and his buddy, Jake, to South Carolina to see Lecrae (Christian hip-hop artist) in concert—our Christmas gift for him that year! We drove through a blizzard for the first hour of the trip. Arriving at our destination in Tega Cay, South Carolina, we stayed with our special friends Gene & Cathy Gaesser—just an hour away from the concert venue. It was an incredibly memorable trip.

The tickets to meet Lecrae before the concert were all sold out which was disappointing. I prayed that we would be able to meet him in person. Drake shared with me that he too prayed that we would have an opportunity to meet Lecrae.

Because the concert was very loud, Cathy and I spent a little time in the hall where we were able to talk to Lecrae's manager. We shared with him how we drove through a blizzard on our ten-hour trip with our twelve-year-old grandson and his friend. He, of course, was excited to hear our story.

The concert ended and as we were standing by the merchandise table, the manager brought Lecrae immediately over to meet Drake and Jake. The manager offered us Lecrae's sweat-drenched T-shirt and asked if the boys wanted it as a souvenir. Of course, they did! When I suggested it be washed, Drake immediately objected and let me know he would take it just as it was.

Once again, we were blessed with not only attending the concert, but God answered the prayers of this young boy to actually meet Lecrae and have the added unexpected treasure of his sweaty T-shirt! What a prize!

To My Grandson, Spencer! Seeing you and your older brothers and sister off on the school bus every morning was always the highlight of my day! As your older siblings went into the higher grades, they graduated to the earlier bus and only you were left for the few short years until you transitioned to the early bus. Breakfast, games we played, the talks were all a part of our mornings. I treasure our times together and thank God everyday for the young man you have grown into my dear Spencer!

Who's Talking?

Just a little boy so precious and sweet
Just a little boy when he stands to his feet
Two little hands that can hold and hug
A grandmother whose there ready to love
These children were precious to her through each year
And now to embrace this one brings much cheer

Help him get ready for school at age six
Watching the clock as it slowly ticks
I speak of God and point spiritual things out
He asks, "Grandma, Is God all you talk about"?
I peer in his eyes with my face close to his
"Can I ask you a question? Will you answer me this"?
"Yes," he replies with so much attention
"Who's talking about God"? I reply with tender affection
"No one Grandma," he says as I nod
"Yes, then I will talk to you about God."

It is God who is so good and so true
Who gave up His life for me and for you
He came to this earth to show us the way

So we can talk to each other day after day
Of life and love and spiritual things
For, dear Spencer, you must learn this…
He is the Lord of all lords
and the King of all kings!

To My Grandson, Colin! You are the youngest of our five grandchildren and the only child in your family which makes you special to so many of us. Caring for you while mommy and daddy worked bonded us closely to each other. The fun, the laughter, the many memories, I hold them very close to my heart. What a joy to watch you grow and mature! God bless you my sweet boy!

"Doose Potty"

We are having a "Doose Potty" as my two-year-old grandson would call it. Colin is such a joy and so full of life! The delicate tea cup would come out and with all the care he could manage at his age, he learned to serve the "doose" from our special teapot.

Our go-to tea cup and saucer had a red rose design that grabbed his attention one day and so began our ritual of having a "Juice Party." It was always with great delight that we would seat ourselves at the dining room table with the cup set and creamer that served as our teapot.

Out would come the phone camera and the video rolled recording our special times at Mimi's house. These videos are a treasure to be sure as the years pass and special little boys grow up.

Nine years old now at this writing, we all get so much joy watching and listening to these memorable times at Mimi's enjoying our "doose" and very fond memories that will always be cherished.
"Doose" anyone?

As Christian Parents, and Grandparents, our roles are not always easy when it comes to having to let go. For years we are the main characters but soon children grow up and our relationship changes. We are not that hub in the wheel any longer but simply a spoke in the wheel.

Spokes are the connecting rods between the hub and the rim. Their main purpose is to transfer the loads between the hub and the rim. Our goal and our attention is always to give of ourselves to not just our families but to our human family expecting nothing in return. We, as empty nesters, have the time to be there for our family and others to help lighten their loads as best we can.

Like a lighthouse, we want to be steadfast and immoveable in our love and our support. Remembering always that "… It is more blessed to give than to receive" (Acts 20:35).

The Lighthouse

God is here establishing, planting—firmly planting
I am here and they are there, adrift on the water
I have not moved—I am where I am—they have gone
But I shall be as a lighthouse firmly planted—unsinkable
Waves crashing all around
But I am not moved—cannot be moved![1]

Light cutting the darkness—a beacon of strength
A refuge in the time of storm
Oh precious light, guiding, shining, steady light
Sword of deliverance—cutting, always cutting the darkness
Looking into the child's eyes, something was wrong
Sadness—shame—confusion? What was it?
Ah, but the lighthouse is here—have no fear my children!

---

[1] *Psalm 107:29 "He stilled the storm to a whisper; the waves of the sea were hushed."*

Here is the light—come towards the light
I have not moved—I will not go away
The light is here—reassuring you—It's OK—It's OK child!
My light is clear and bright—it has not moved
I am here my children—oh beloved children of my heart
Precious ones—be at peace—I speak peace—I am here!
For God is here—He is always here
With light for this lighthouse![2]

<hr>

[2] *I John 1:5 "… God is light; in him there is no darkness at all."*

Part Five

Let Go of Brokenness...
Hold On To Your
HEART

Journal Entry: I love this quote—"Our greatest glory is not in never failing but in rising up every time we fail" (Ralph Waldo Emerson). As we face the good and the not-so-good in life, we realize how totally vulnerable we are to our circumstances. It is at that pivotal point that those happenings can make us or break us. I understand more than ever that we can, even in our brokenness, rise to a new awareness of the often-difficult situations that can trap us. As we come to this new level of awareness, we can surrender to a greater power working in us. That, my friends, is the redemptive power of a loving, awe-inspiring God.

The Mosaic

Pieces, nothing but pieces
Broken, scattered pieces all around me
Sharp, jagged pieces lying at my feet
Barefoot and vulnerable, I don't know where to turn
Trapped and frozen in this place of disconnection
With no one to help me and no one who really cares.
I cower in this place of brokenness
This place of aloneness

This place of misery—with my back against a wall
I sink down to the lowest level of despair
In my sinking, I examine the pieces
As I examine the fragments in my hand
I rise up and face my wall—my barrier
Can I piece things back together again?
Can I move back to a time when the pieces were whole?
What could I have done to prevent this shattering?

Life is so fragile…so delicate…so intricately formed
Just like humpty dumpty sitting on his wall
No power on earth could put together the pieces again
I face my wall, picking up each piece one by one
The path clear now, I am able to move again
I step back for a better view
I step back again—still a little obscure…
As I distance myself, the picture is clearer

What I see is a miracle before me
The mosaic, made of all the broken pieces,
is bright and beautiful
It's drawing power is soothing,
Calming with purpose and meaning
The message is clear, the message is strong
The message is one of beauty and worth
To the one who struggles, it is a message of hope

For the one who has lost at life must always remember
The encouraging story this mosaic weaves
Not just a story of pain, heartache, and brokenness
But ultimately, an artistic work of beauty and grace
It's time to let go—time to face our walls that stop us
They stand so tall and firm—immovable
Learning to turn over our struggles to a heavenly power
To all of God's mercy and grace

Letting go of all bitterness and strife and malice
Facing our walls and beholding the beauty
of all our broken pieces
Telling a story too precious for words!

Tears In a Bottle

Why, oh why, you ask, where, oh where is God?
So much abandonment, flailing from day-to-day
Misunderstood oh so misunderstood
Life passing by without the turn of a head
Does He not see? Does He not notice?
Why, oh why, you ask, where, oh where is God?

I am here, comes the answer
I was there in your betrayal
I was there in your confusion
I was there in your rebellion
I was there in the beatings
I was there in the abuse
I was there in your searching
I was there all along.

The road was obscure, and your steps were unsure
But I was there leading the way
There with the love you longed to know
There with the security and the assurance that all is well
There to sustain you, there to comfort and be with you
There to catch your tears every time you cried.

Every teardrop is so precious to me
I keep them you know stored away in a bottle[1]
To pour out upon you when you are dry
They soften the heart—they do!
And I want to remind you
That for those tears I died.

---

[1] *Psalm 56:8 "You number my wanderings; put my tears into Your bottle; are they not in Your book?" (NKJV)*

Note: Though my Father was very difficult through my years at home, he really mellowed in his "grandfather" years. I very much enjoyed him in my adult years and was grateful to see the loving part of his heart that endeared him to us all!

Journal Entry: June 17, 2017

As I listened to a teaching on writing poetry, the speaker suggested an exercise to write about a memory of something that was painful in our childhood. I immediately thought of the abuse. I was about six years old when I was at a public pool and I realized my father's handprint was on the top of my shoulder. In today's culture, with child abuse awareness at an all-time high, someone probably would have reported this to the authorities.

I grew up desperately wanting to feel safe and secure and most of all wanting to be loved. I have spent years on trying to understand what would possess a parent to be so harmful. As a mother and grandmother, I cannot imagine anger that would lead to such cruelty. But who knows what kind of a mother I would have been had I not turned over my life to Jesus when I was 24 and mother of a four-year-old and an infant. I only know that when I became spiritually conscious, the rage disappeared and love and peace filled my soul for the first time in my life. REALLY!!!

REALLY!?!

The sting of the blows across my body
The imprint of your hand on my shoulder
Hiding from your wrath under my bed
What did I do that deserved such cruelty? REALLY!?!
Did you not know that I just yearned for your love?
Yearned for your acceptance—for your attention?

I was so little—REALLY!?!
What could I have done to deserve such abuse?
I needed to feel safe and secure
Just wanted to be happy
Happy to call you my daddy
To feel safe in this family

I always knew I was not valued
My younger sister was your favorite
You actually told me that in my 40's
Wow! REALLY!?! Was I not your daughter too?
I was so good—always wanted to please
Always needing to be accepted—to be valued—to be loved

As a teenager, I looked for love in all the wrong places
In all the wrong ways
Rebellion crept in like a stealth bomber
Ready to blow up, obliterate, blot out
This gentle, beautiful child
Who just wanted to be accepted, to be valued, to be loved!
REALLY!!!

After the Funeral

Well, Buba, you are gone from this earth
This place you called home
Gone from my life
But you were never really in my life
Trust me when I say I loved you
Or should I say I wanted to
With all of my heart, I wanted to feel secure
I wanted to be a great daughter to you
But you never let me

The memories of you beating me when I was so young…
I would hide under the bed—so afraid you would find me
Why were you always so angry with me?
My only desire was to please you and Ma
I longed for peace in our home but there was none
Doing my best to help was all I strived for
To feel secure and be loved was all I wanted
The day came when I couldn't try to please you any longer
You filled a beautiful heart with bitterness and rebellion

I was never a priority to you—never the focus
You robbed me of the joy of my childhood
You robbed me of the joy of a relationship with my Father
But thank God! What was intended for my destruction
God turned for good in my life
As a young mother with my infant and four-year-old
My Heavenly Father stepped in with love—PURE love

He filled my heart and displaced the darkness
Replaced the heaviness with peace

I had never experienced love and peace like that!
Felt totally accepted—totally valuable
That love that came with my encounter with Jesus
It more than enabled me to, in turn, love others
I can say with all of my heart that I forgive you
For God saved the things in me that were precious
The heart that no one appreciated was redeemed
He stood with me—never rejected me
But pulled me close to His heart

It was there that I began to see the beauty of my life
The turmoil was turned into a timely treasure
Beautiful pearls were formed through the irritations
I don't fault you and I am grateful that you mellowed
I thank God that the curse over this family is broken
My children and the generations to follow can be free
Love and truth prevail over any form of evil or ill-will
Buba, I proclaim over your children—my siblings
That bondages are broken from the sin of past generations

I pray that your soul has found rest
That you have reunited with your family and friends
Who have gone before you
Jesus died that you may come face-to-face with Him
Who died that you may have eternal life
Who died that we as your seed would be at peace
I pray that God's Kingdom of love will come
Into the hearts of those you have left behind.
Rest in peace, Buba! I love you!

Journal Entry: August 2, 2017

Through our difficult life experiences, we can feel betrayed or abandoned. In these times of testing, it can be an opportunity to really examine what we are feeling and truly look at how we react. These negative encounters can reveal the depth of brokenness in us.

The good news is that each trial we go through, brings us closer to the truth about ourselves. It's not strength I find in and of myself. It is learning to lean on and look to the One who holds our hearts in His hands. God can lead us along a path of healing and wholeness.

We need to allow these "disturbances" that can throw us off balance to be a light shining on our inner wounds. We can't be healed unless we are aware of the brokenness. Each negative experience we encounter can strengthen us to understand ourselves more and move on to a quicker recovery. Healing is a process. It is available to us as we are on our knees with our heads lifted.

Knees Down, Head Lifted

Slammed against the wall
Trapped with no way out
Dropping to her knees
She seeks, she prays, she waits
As her knees go down
Her head lifts up
Her heart is open.

She can see up above the storm clouds
High above powers and principalities[1]
Forces that want to snuff her out
Always trying to destroy
To distract, to diminish
The one whose knees are down
And whose head is lifted.

She's learned there is comfort in this place
Pain and heartache casting her down
A gift from above from the All-Knowing One
Who is shaping and forming this frail one
As she goes down, strength comes in
In this place of nothingness,
She finds her everything.

In this place, strife gives way to peace
In her aloneness, she learns she is never alone
So with knees down and head lifted,
Contentment comes
The dead end is a new beginning
She hears, "Peace! Be Still!"
It is truly well with her again.

---

[1] *Ephesians 6:12 "For our fight is not against flesh and blood, but against principalities, against powers, against the rulers of the darkness of this world…"*

Note: For all of us who have struggled with family relationships, take heart! Hold on when you need to and have the wisdom to let go when you must!

Back story for "My Siblings"

It was in the mid-nineties, almost three decades ago, that I remember first confronting my sister. She had come from Indiana to visit our parents. When I entered the home I asked her and my parents why they never let me know she was coming. After that confrontation, I thought things would change but they never did.

They continued to keep me out of their gatherings. I was also not invited to our mother's 90th birthday party.

It's interesting how the narcissistic, controlling tendencies that seemed to be engrained in my parents were showing up big time in my younger siblings.

Through it all, I realized that God used it powerfully in my life. There was an intense gratitude and understanding that began to take shape within my heart as I learned to let go.

The Bible is filled with story after story of how God always used rejection to draw his people closer to Himself. For years, my prayer in every difficulty was "It's OK Lord!" Through the years, it became easier and easier to let go.

To accept with joy life's difficulties is truly a gift. The triggers that so many times controlled me were soon becoming a thing of the past. The progression that is evident in "My Siblings" transpired over years of work on myself. For this I am forever indebted to my younger siblings…!!

My Siblings

As if on purpose, you left me out
As if on purpose, you did not call
As if on purpose, you did not notice
That I was sinking deep in a pool of bitterness
The wounds feel fresh though they are old
Older than me—before my years

As if on purpose, you did not look
As if on purpose, you did not talk
As if on purpose, you did not wonder
You did not try to feel where I really was
I talked, but you did not hear me
Words so unimportant—so misunderstood

As if on purpose, I did not come
As if on purpose, I stood my ground
As if on purpose, I wiped you out
I hardened my heart and dried my eyes
No longer important to me and my world
I did not care—I could not

As if on purpose, I lifted my eyes
As if on purpose, I prayed for you
As if on purpose, the peace did come
Reassurance of division and not unity
The sword—not peace was the promise[1]
Of a life that is to be lost—then found!

---

[1] *Matthew 10:34-40 "Do not think that I came to bring peace on the earth; I did not
come to bring peace, but a sword…and a person's enemies will be the members of his
household."*

As if on purpose, I saw a greater plan
As if on purpose, my priorities had shifted
As if on purpose, my heart was free
Free to pick up my pearls and clean off the mud[2]
Free and able to be sent to others
Knowing that what was meant for evil,
God turned to the good![3]

---

[2] *Matthew 7:6 "Do not give what is holy to dogs, and do not throw your pearls before pigs, or they will trample them under their feet, and turn and tear you to pieces."*

[3] *Genesis 50:20 "As for you, you meant evil against me, but God meant it for good in order to bring about this present result, to preserve many people alive."*

The Confrontation

She feels empty, she feels free
The hungry ghost that lived in her
Is no longer there
Always filling, filling, filling
But never feeling full
At last relief from constant pursuit
Of love and happiness

A place of belonging
Is what she's been looking for
But even more there's been striving
This beast inside always driving
Always pushing her—needing more

Insatiable beast of self
Subdued here for a while
At this place of confrontation
Feeling of a weened child
Not needing to matter, she is content to be empty
And the emptiness fills every nook and cranny.
And now she sits content and at peace!

A Window Called Time

Weep on oh willow for you have cause
Your trunks and branches have fallen
Lifeless limbs drop like leaves
The winds have blown
Strong winds—powerful winds
Reducing you to a mere shadow
Of what once stood strong—Stood firm and immovable.

The shade you once offered
And the limbs and trunks
That young hearts were compelled to explore
Are forever gone…
Gone with only reflections and shadows
Of a time when you stood beautiful and serene
With a majesty, all your own

I will always remember you, oh willow!
Perhaps from a sense of oneness with you
For I too stood strong once—immovable

But life's winds have blown
Strong winds—powerful winds
Time reducing me to a mere shadow
From strength to weakness.

The grass withers, the flowers fade[1]
All things must come to an end

---

[1] *Isaiah 40:8 "The grass withers, the flower fades, but the word of our God stands forever."*

For life like nature consists of seasons[2]
Seasons that come and go
Constantly changing
Not meant to last forever
But to be embraced in this window called time.

---

[2] *Ecclisiastes 3:1 "The grass withers, the flower fades, when the breath of the Lord blows upon it; The people are indeed grass."*

To This Generation

Let me love you in the most perfect way
Put arms around you to relieve all your pain
Till all is settled and at peace deep within
And hope is renewed like a sweet long lost friend
Oh receive this love from a heart that is pure
Come, find the strength that will help you endure
Whatever it is that is causing the grief
Lay down your load and find some relief

"Come to Me," is the invitation to those who are weary
Find rest for your souls for life can be dreary
Take His yoke and learn—He is gentle and meek[1]
Truth will be found by those who will seek[2]
Your help will come just look up to the hills
He turns mourning to dancing and comes and He fills
The heart that is broken and cumbered with pain
To count all things loss for Christ is the gain.[3]

---

[1] *Matthew 11:28-30 "Come to Me, all who are weary and burdened, and I will give you rest."*

[2] *Jeremiah 29:13 "And you will seek Me and find Me when you search for Me with all your heart."*

[3] *Philippians 3:8 "More than that, I count all things to be loss in view of the surpassing value of knowing Christ Jesus my Lord, for whom I have suffered the loss of all things, and count them mere rubbish, so that I may gain Christ."*

Sydney Paige

The heart and the hand of a child
There is no greater gift
A heart full of love spilling over
Splashing all around me
Amazing love—this pure, undefiled treasure
So spotless and pure
Brings so much comfort to my wounded heart
Extends a hand—a little hand
A precious hand
A hand to hold
A love to cherish

Thank you, my new little friend
For the gift you have given
You are a pure delight
May that gift of love and friendship
Never diminish
Keep your heart full
Keep your hand extended
And reaching…

Dear Friend

Thank you for this place of rejection
I desire this place of nothingness
Its brokenness compels me to come
Pushing, birthing, forming
Bringing freedom from pride and self
Welcome dear sweet rejection

Into this lowly place I come
When I'm riding high
My horse goes out from under me
I see myself in the truth of the mirage
The dreams vanish and hopes are dashed

Make me nothing oh beautiful place of nothingness
Make me empty oh still place of shattered dreams
Make me not elate myself in the honor of men
But truly let me honor all that brokenness brings
It is not my work not my will
It is this broken place I love

Take me out of my own thinking[1]
Remove all of my thoughts
It is this glorious place of nothingness that I desire
That I long to walk in and be content in
This beautiful realm of rejection
I embrace you, dear friend!

---

[1] *John 3:30 "He must increase, but I must decrease."*

The Maze

Accept the work, accept the work
In the darkness, the problems overwhelm
In a tunnel, in a maze, lost again

But through the darkness, a light appears
A light appears at the end of this tunnel
Moving toward it, things a little clearer

Focus, don't get distracted by different paths
Lead on! Lead on! Oh perfect light
Follow, follow—always follow

Moving closer, the way gets brighter
Clearer now by the brilliance of this light
Another emerges from the darkness of this tunnel
Emerging—forever changed
Subdued—at peace in the light
Offering light and life to help others through the maze.

Tricked

You tricked her oh delusional life
You've caused her to stumble
To wonder about life and love
How could she have been so blind
Love as cold as steal in sub-zero temperatures
Mother, father, brothers, sister,
Fractured relationships with no comfort

She emerges from this rubble
Brushing off the cold and heartless
And finds herself in a new place
With colors as warm as the sun
Finding brightness and light shining
In all the once blackened dark corners
Magnificent light although blinding at first

The eyes adjust and understanding comes
To see clearly and to accept all that is laid bare
And made visible by the light
Feeling like a weened child
The wanting, wishing and hoping pass
Acceptance and serenity now shield the strengthened heart
Never to be tricked again.

It's All About

It's all about the weak, the small and the abused
It's all about healing the broken-hearted
The desolate ones, the alone and rejected

It's all about never giving up
But letting go of those things that are destructive
The anger, the bitterness, the fear.

It's all about reaching out with kindness and love
It's all about the making of a champion
The making of a man, woman, and child

It's all about being affected by life's circumstances
And letting destiny have its way
Letting compassion and love heal all of the brokenness

It's all about bringing healing to the broken
It's all about looking forward to the new,
The healed, the secure

It's all about being whole
It's all about…

Note: The following piece was written at an acting workshop I attended on April 30, 2002. We were asked to write about ourselves. It's interesting that I ended with "Hello Nina" since I did not refer to myself by that name. It really surprised me that I wrote that ending.

My birth name is "Antonina." Since I was born in Sicily, I suppose in an effort to Americanize my name, I was registered in Kindergarten as "Anna" which brought a lot of confusion to my young mind. As a teenager, I officially changed my name to "Ann" when I was sworn in as a citizen of the United States.

In 2007, my father died. Wishing to return to my roots and tired of having two names ("Nina" to family and close friends and "Ann" to co-workers and in public), I asked that everyone call me "Nina," which they did. I feel very comfortable as "Nina" and it suits me well. I finally feel good about my name and I celebrate me!

Hatching

I feel like I've come through a fearful place
Controlled by those around me
Never able to come to the real me
The me that I've been
Even before me was conscious
Coming closer to who I am
Egg hatching
Dreams birthing... Wings spreading...
Flying... Soaring... A new world opening up
Discovering freedom where once was bondage
New confidence where once was insecurity
New day dawning
Sun rising... Brightness... Wholeness... Fearless
Hello me!
Hello, *Nina*

About the Author

While balancing family and career many doors of opportunity opened through the years giving Antonina Caprino Bell, also known as Nina, experience on a national and international level in the business and ministry arena. The highlight of her career included a position with Concerned Women for America in Washington, D.C. as Field Development Coordinator.

With 15 years in the school system, 18 years as a mentor under Big Brother Big Sister Program, and years of experience with youth groups, Nina has a passion for youth and works hard to pass the baton on to the next generation. Currently, she is a nationally certified instructor for the R.E.A.L. Essentials Program (Relationship Education and Leadership) in schools throughout the county.

Nina is an avid volunteer in the community serving as Board member of Nonprofit organizations including the UCAN City Mission. She is the Founder and Director of Women of EnCOURAGEment, a ministry under the umbrella of The Better Place, Inc. of which she has served as a Board Member since 2010.

Nina views herself as just an ordinary person in the hands of an extraordinary God! The timeless message through her writing and speaking is a message of hope and healing through faith in God. Married in 1969, Nina resides in Western New York with her husband, Russ. They have three sons and five grandchildren.